Dairy

BY ALLISON LASSIEUR

amicus
high interest

Amicus High Interest is an imprint of Amicus
P.O. Box 1329, Mankato, MN 56002
www.amicuspublishing.us

Library of Congress Cataloging-in-Publication Data
Lassieur, Allison.
 Dairy / by Allison Lassieur.
    pages cm. — (Where does our food come from?)
Audience: K to grade 3.
Includes bibliographical references and index.
 Summary: "Describes dairy foods, an essential part of a
healthy diet, including where different animals are raised,
why dairy foods are healthy for us, and how other parts of
the world consume dairy foods"— Provided by publisher.
 ISBN 978-1-60753-499-0 (library binding) —
 ISBN 978-1-60753-706-9 (ebook)
 1. Dairying—Juvenile literature. 2. Dairy products—Juvenile
literature. I. Title.
 SF239.5.L37 2015
 636.2'142—dc23
                                        2013035391

Editors   Rebecca Glaser and Tram Bui
Series Designer   Kathleen Petelinsek
Book Designer   Heather Dreisbach
Photo Researcher   Kurtis Kinneman

Photo Credits: Monkey Business Images, cover; Elena
Schweitzer/Shutterstock, 5; Photographee.eu/Shutterstock, 6;
Cultura Limited/SuperStock, 9; Marco Govel/Shutterstock, 10;
Peter Horree/Alamy, 13; Belinda Pretorius/Dreamstime, 14;
Clover/SuperStock, 17; FLPA/SuperStock, 18; John Warburton
Lee/SuperStock, 21; E.A. Janes/age fotostock/SuperStock, 22;
Nomad/SuperStock, 25; Asia Images/SuperStock, 26; Blend
Images/Alamy, 29

Printed in the United States of America at Corporate Graphics
in North Mankato, Minnesota.

10 9 8 7 6 5 4 3 2 1

Table of Contents

What Is Dairy?

How are cheese, ice cream, and pudding alike? They all taste great. But that is not it. All these foods are dairy foods. Dairy foods are foods made from milk. And they are alike in another way. Dairy foods all have a **nutrient** called **calcium**. Calcium makes your bones and teeth hard and strong.

Ice cream is made from milk.

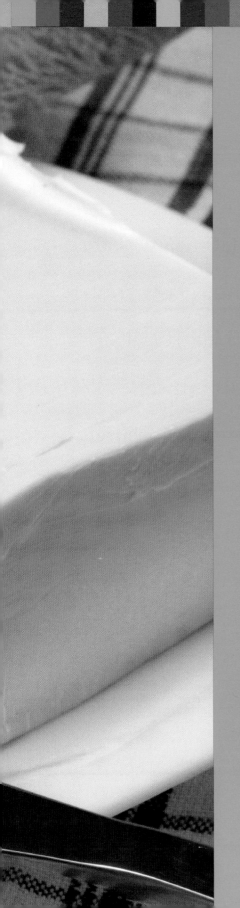

Butter, cream, and cream cheese are made from milk. But they are not in the dairy food group. Why is that? They do not have a lot of calcium. The calcium goes away when these foods are made. They are fats. They are still good for us to eat, but just in small amounts.

Butter is good in small amounts.

Dairy foods have a lot of fat. Many dairy foods have the fat taken out. Have you ever heard of skim milk? That is milk with the fat taken out. You can eat low-fat cheese or low-fat yogurt. Dairy that is not low-fat can be good for you, too. Our bodies need healthy fats to grow.

 How did skim milk get its name?

Skim milk is a good, low-fat dairy food.

 The fat, or cream, is "skimmed" off the top of the milk.

9

Cows are milked to make dairy foods.

Where Do Dairy Foods Come From?

Most dairy foods in America are made with cows' milk. Some of it is sold as milk and cream. The rest is made into foods like cheese and yogurt. Some people cannot eat foods made with cows' milk. It makes them sick. They eat dairy foods made with soymilk.

Dairy cows start every day with breakfast. Then the farmer milks them. After that, they go out to the fields. The cows eat grass all day. They also eat hay, grains, and other foods. It makes the milk taste good. The cows go back to the barn in the afternoon for a second milking.

 How much milk does one cow make?

A machine milks cows at a dairy farm. It happens two times each day.

 One cow can make 2,300 gallons (8,706 liters) of milk every year. That is enough to fill 25 bathtubs with milk.

Goats can make milk
just like cows can.

Cows make lots of milk. But other animals make milk, too. People drink milk from goats and sheep. Goats' milk has lots of calcium. It makes soft, creamy cheese. Most sheep's milk is made into cheese, too. Sheep's milk is also made into ice cream and yogurt.

Dairy Around the Corner

You do not have to go far to see a dairy farm. Every state has dairy farms. They deliver most of their milk to local stores. Dairy farms have a lot of black and white cows. They are **Holsteins**. They are the best dairy cows. Holsteins make more milk than any other cow.

Cows live on dairy farms in every state.

Milk is moved in special tanks. They make sure the milk stays cold.

Q How long does it take for milk to get from the cow to the store?

Dairy cows are milked with big milking machines. The fresh milk goes into big tanks. The tanks keep the milk cold. Soon the milk is loaded onto a truck. The truck takes the milk to a **processing plant**. The milk goes into cartons and jugs. Then it goes to the store.

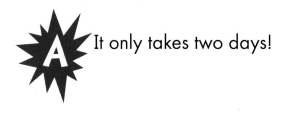 It only takes two days!

Dairy Around the World

People around the world eat dairy foods. But their milk does not always come from cows. Some places are not good for cows to live. Goats can live in places that cows can't. Most people around the world drink goats' milk. You can find goats' milk in the United States, too. Some stores sell goats' milk cheese.

 What is the most popular dairy product in the world?

These children take care of their goat herd. The goats make milk.

 Cheese. There are hundreds of types of cheese.

Water buffalo live in India. People in India drink water buffalo milk. Half of the milk in India comes from water buffalo. Water buffalo do not like to be milked. They do not make much milk. But their milk tastes very good. It makes great cheese.

Water buffalo make milk, too. People in India drink it.

Many other animals give milk. Reindeer live in cold countries. People in those countries drink reindeer milk. They make reindeer cheese. Yaks make milk, too! People in Tibet make tea with yak milk. Yak tea has a salty taste. They also make yak cheese and yak butter.

 Are there other animals that make milk?

People can get their milk from yaks!

 All mammals do, even humans!

Healthy Dairy

Dairy foods are part of a healthy diet. They have calcium. Calcium is good for your bones and teeth. Dairy foods also help your heart. Milk has protein and **vitamin D**. Vitamin D helps your body use calcium. Vitamin D and calcium work together. They make your body strong.

Children who drink milk have strong bones.

How much dairy is good for you? Young kids should eat 2½ cups (625 mL) of dairy foods every day. What counts as a cup? Two slices of cheddar cheese count. So does a glass of milk, soymilk, or a cup of yogurt. Even ice cream counts, but it has less calcium than milk and cheese. Eat foods from all the food groups to stay healthy and grow.

 If you don't eat dairy foods, how can you get calcium?

Ice cream is a yummy summer treat. And it gives you some calcium.

 Some non-dairy foods, such as soybeans and canned fish, have calcium. Some orange juice has calcium added.

Glossary

calcium A nutrient found in dairy foods.

Holstein A black and white dairy cow.

nutrient A chemical that keeps the body healthy.

processing plant A place where food is made healthy for us to eat.

vitamin D A chemical that helps your body use calcium.

Read More

Clark, Katie. *The Dairy Group*. Mankato, Minn.: Child's World, 2013.

Cleary, Brian. *Yogurt and Cheeses and Ice Cream That Pleases*. Minneapolis: Millbrook Press, 2011.

Schuh, Mari. *Dairy on MyPlate*. Mankato, Minn.: Capstone Press, 2013.

Websites

Cool Dairy Facts
www.greenmeadowfarms.com/cooldairyfacts.htm

Eating Well with Canada's Food Guide
www.hc-sc.gc.ca/fn-an/food-guide-aliment/index-eng.php

MooMilk: A Dynamic Adventure into the Dairy Industry
www.moomilk.com

MyPlate Kids' Place
www.choosemyplate.gov/kids/index.html

Every effort has been made to ensure that these websites are appropriate for children. However, because of the nature of the Internet, it is impossible to guarantee that these sites will remain active indefinitely or that their contents will not be altered.

Index

About the Author

Allison Lassieur tries to eat plenty of fresh, good foods at every meal. She has written more than 100 books for kids. Allison especially likes to write about history, food, and science. She lives in a house in the woods with her husband, daughter, three dogs, two cats, and a blue fish named Marmalade.